# MOST

## *Valuable*

# DAVID CHANEY

Cover Design: Scott Soliz, www.zealdesino.com
ISBN 13: 979-8465191562

3741106NC_Sep24

# Dedication

I would like to dedicate this book to my team of advisors at Legacy Planning Partners LLC. First, I would like to acknowledge my father, Mike Chaney. Without his fifty plus years of dedicated leadership and thoughtful mentorship our firm would not exist as it does today. Second, I would like to thank my daughter Madison Chaney for helping me continue our legacy of helping families protect and preserve their legacies for generations to come. Next, I must congratulate my sister in-law and Madison's aunt, Teresa Howard for her tenth-year anniversary of helping our clients construct and maintain their Family Legacy constitutions. Next, I would like acknowledge Matt Pendergrass for his tireless work and long hours spent helping our firm maintain superior service to our clients. Finally, I would like to express my appreciation to Anthony Hernandez for joining me twenty-five years ago and working with me to grow and protect the assets entrusted to our firm.

# Contents

# Foreword

About ten years ago, I was introduced to David by a mutual friend of ours, and shortly after, we met up to discuss his involvement in the planning of our family estate. Going into the meeting, I assumed we would just be talking about the details of our stuff, discussing our investments and reviewing our life insurance policy and our revocable living trust. We did some of that; however, I was surprised by the connection we had with David on the importance of intentionally creating and passing an inheritance that goes beyond our stuff. We discussed the importance of a legacy by design, not by default, which passes on our valuables, our vision, our values, our virtues, and our village. Just like building a great financial plan doesn't happen by accident, legacy by design requires making an investment, paying attention, and taking the time.

In that meeting, we realized our common passion and burden to help others accomplish a great legacy, not just a great inheritance of financial wealth. David has not only been an excellent financial and estate planning adviser, he has also been a friend whom I can truly trust to give wise counsel. I can honestly tell you that my relationship with David has been invaluable to me, my family and our future generations.

Thank you, David, for your investment in me and all those who come behind me.

-Brian Hill, TheCedarGate.com

# Chapter 1
# Values Before Money

If you gave ten million dollars to each of your kids right now, what do you think would happen?

Would they lose touch with reality and blow it all on Ferraris, yachts, and partying? Would they be mature enough to invest it in real estate, the stock market, or a business startup? Would they be generous enough to give a portion away? Would they try to handle it with the best intentions but just end up wasting it due to lack of experience? Would they be wise enough to seek the council of others? Would they be disciplined enough to not destroy their life?

Most important of all, would they use it in a way that honors the kind of legacy you want to leave?

Every loving parent wants to bless their kids with good gifts, but it takes special care and a plan to ensure the gift does not become a curse. Growing up the son of an estate planner for wealthy families, I saw every size of gift you can imagine, and I was constantly astonished at how something as wonderful as an inheritance can so easily turn into such a catastrophic mess when not properly planned for.

I started with Dad's financial and estate planning firm when I was twenty-five-years-old. I shadowed Dad for the first month, getting to visit clients with him and meet some of the wealthiest people in Oklahoma and their children. Many of those children, thirty or forty years old, were in positions to start developing estate planning for themselves, which meant they were ideal client prospects for me. And that beat the heck out of my original prospect circle of broke college friends.

Have you ever heard it said, "Some of the wealthiest people in the world are also the most miserable"? I used to wonder how that was possible. But in my mid-twenties, as I started working with my new clients and becoming friends with them, I was about to learn.

Jeremy was a client of mine. He was thirty years old, drove a flashy sports car, lived in a mansion in one of the wealthy neighborhoods in Oklahoma City, and did whatever he wanted all day, every day. He was the child of one of my dad's clients, and a new client for me. He lived the life so many people only dream of. Every month, a 20,000 dollar check arrived in his mailbox from the trust fund created by his family.

What a gift, right? I mean, who wouldn't want a 20,000 dollar monthly check from their parents' or grandparents' trust fund? Well, not so fast.

Jeremy lived a life that would be envied by many, yet he was deeply depressed. Within a year of him becoming my client, Jeremy committed suicide. He wasn't the only client I lost to death, either. Another client of mine drank himself to death while another overdosed on drugs.

"What is wrong with these people?" I wondered. "How do you have everything you could ever want, and yet be so empty and depressed you commit suicide?" As I came to learn, it's not having material possessions that makes us miserable, but rather, never learning to value and work for what we have.

A colleague of mine, Dr. Campbell, worked with our firm quite a bit. He's a psychologist, but we told our clients that he was a "family communication specialist" because some people don't want to meet with a psychologist. I asked him one day why he thought so many wealthy heirs were so miserable. He told me that when somebody gives you something, oftentimes it creates a lack of self-awareness, self-fulfillment, and self-esteem.

"Self-esteem doesn't come easy," Dr. Campbell said. "No one can *give* it to you, it's something you have to build based on your own accomplishments."

I've come to think of it like this: when you were a kid and built a car out of Legos, you felt accomplished, right? You valued it and wanted to show it off to your friends, because *you* did that, even if your parents were the ones who bought you the set and taught you how to assemble it. But, if your parents built it all for you,

you felt cheated somehow. Why? Because the satisfaction and pride that comes with accomplishing something yourself was stolen from you.

Today, I believe that equipping our kids with the knowledge, opportunities, and tools to succeed is a beautiful thing. But when parents eliminate the need to succeed, the blessing becomes a curse.

When I came into the business, my dad's client base was many of the who's who of the Oklahoma oil boom. Their focus was on tax avoidance, and we would help these families plan to leave even more wealth for their kids and less wealth to the government. This sounds great, but in the end, I felt that it just made the problems worse since the more money you pass on, the bigger mess it can turn your family into. If all I was doing was helping people make generational catastrophes, maybe I should focus on asset management more than estate planning.

But then, I heard something that changed the way I saw everything.

There was a financial planning conference in Seattle, Washington, that my dad wanted me to attend with him. Nick Murray—a known author and speaker to money management advisors—was speaking at the conference, so I agreed to go. One afternoon, we attended a session led by a financial group from Walla Walla, Washington.

One of the things the Walla Walla group talked about was the responsibility of estate planners to not only help our clients pass their wealth to their kids, but also their *values*—the ideologies, beliefs, and principles most important to them. They went on to explain that the most valuable asset that we have as entrepreneurs is our value system. If we can pass that value system of how to create wealth, respect and manage wealth, and do great things with that wealth, then we don't have to worry about how many material possessions we pass to the next generation. With the right value systems, each generation will be able to handle that wealth and build their own.

"What if we could do that?" I wondered. "What if

we could help people not just pass their money, but also pass and protect those things that are the most valuable of all?"

David Green, founder and CEO of Hobby Lobby, captures the same idea in his book, *A Generous Life:* "Wealth transfer is not just about money. In our Green family document, we define wealth as 'intellectual, social, financial, and spiritual capital.' In passing on a legacy to the next generation, I want to pass on more than just financial wealth."

Years later, I have learned from mentors and experience that wealth is neither destructive nor constructive—it is neutral. The difference is in how you lay the foundation.

There are two core pillars in transferring wealth from generation to generation: a strong values system, and strategic planning to keep it strong. If done correctly, the wealth you leave your family will not hinder their growth as human beings. Instead, it can actually accelerate them in life faster, higher, and further because they have access to resources that many people don't have for the first half or third of their life. It can be a head-start rather than a stumbling block.

The question, then, is how do you use wealth to lay a strong foundation for your family?

What is your greatest asset?

Before the conference in Washington, most of my clients would have answered that question with a statement of their bank account, their company, or their stock portfolio. But one of the ideas the estate planning group from Walla Walla asserted was that people's greatest assets are not their things. Now, I ask that question a different way:

What is most valuable to you?

Your relationships? Your integrity? Your faith? Your convictions? Your vision? And yes, your money is certainly on the list of things valuable to you, but where on this list does it go? Does it take first place, or is money only as valuable as the growth and strength it lends to the other things that matter most?

There's a joke that says, "He who dies with the most stuff wins." It sounds absurd, right? But it's how so many of us live. The most common factor I've found in unhappy, wealthy people is their worship of money and material things. It is not the money itself that makes them unhappy, but the fact that they've placed their self-worth and identity in the amount of money they possess.

The Bible says, "Where your treasure is, there your heart is also," (Matthew 6:21). If you treasure objects, that's where your heart is. But if you treasure people, relationships, and values, that will be where your heart is.

Over and over again, I find the families that are broken and struggling are ones who have received wealth with an absence of values and self-worth. The greatest gift and inheritance we can leave our family is a healthy value system that can be instilled in future generations. A healthy value system not only teaches how to create and use wealth, but also what is important to know and believe about wealth.

I hope to accomplish two things in this book: I want to equip you to be smart in the way you approach transferring your wealth to future generations, and to challenge you to be intentional about the values you are passing on. No amount of smart financial management ever replaces fundamental values. It takes both to leave a lasting legacy. If you are a parent who wants to make sure your gift grows into a healthy, flourishing legacy for your kids and not a debilitating mess, this book is for you.

What kind of legacy do you want to leave?

# Chapter 2
# Intentional
# Legacy

We do not choose the cards we are dealt in life, but we do choose the legacy we leave behind. But choosing your legacy is not as easy as choosing your favorite pizza toppings. We don't get to say, "I want that legacy," hit purchase, and kick back and wait for it to be delivered to your house. Choosing your legacy requires vigorous intentionality in the choices you make every single day, and it takes more than good intentions—it takes a plan.

How do we be intentional? Allow me to tell you two different stories really quick. Both true, but with distortions and crossovers of other stories to protect privacy.

The first story starts off with the Cooper family. As a successful entrepreneur, Mr. Cooper was excited to leave behind the opportunities and lifestyle for his future generations he worked so hard for. His son was a disciplined, stable man whom Mr. Cooper trusted completely to receive his inheritance in a healthy way. However, he was concerned about the erratic patterns of his daughter's husband. He opted to safeguard her half of the inheritance with specific conditions in his planning.

In time, Mr. Cooper died, and his two children received their halves of the inheritance—the son received it outright, and the daughter received access to his money only under certain spendthrift conditions designed to preserve wealth. She could borrow from the trust, make withdrawals for education and medical bills, and access it in dozens of different ways, but not in a way that would jeopardize future generation's needs.

Sadly, several years later, Mr. Cooper's son was diagnosed with cancer at the young age of fifty and passed away. With no wife at the time, his half of the inheritance was left completely unchecked to his three young adult children. Just imagine if you had five million dollars dropped in your lap at twenty-four-years-old! Would you have kept your head on straight? Maybe, but don't act like it wouldn't have been hard!

In the case of the Cooper grandchildren, they completely lost their minds. They quit their jobs, dropped out of school, and rolled around in their money like it was everything they could ever want. Five million dollars each went up in smoke in a few short years, leaving the grandchildren broke, uneducated, and with no future ahead of them.

On the other side of the family, things went differently.

Because of the wealth preservation planning, Mr. Cooper's daughter and her husband were measured in their access to the money, and by extension, their own kids were also limited. Today, the daughter's trust account has grown from fifteen million dollars to forty million dollars.

Just something to think about: your son or daughter may not need conditions and restraints on their inheritance, but your grandkids might!

In the second story, we meet Mr. and Mrs. Jones. Also successful entrepreneurs, this couple has been a client of mine for years. I've had the honor of helping them plan their legacy and watching it in action.

They have three kids. In the last ten years, each of the kids have been able to take the money they borrowed from their dad's family bank (more on "family banks" in a minute) and build businesses that are extremely successful today.

The oldest son built a company that had a net profit last year of 1.6 million dollars. The daughter founded a multimillion-dollar company that now employs between 400 and 500 people. The youngest son built a company that he has since sold. As a result, he has been able to contribute five million dollars to his own family bank.

All of this was possible because, instead of enabling their children with upscale lifestyles that they never had to earn, Mr. and Mrs. Jones focused on *empowering* their kids to succeed on their own. They made a deal with each of their kids that once their business became profitable, they would forgive the loans if they would put half of the profits into their own family bank for their own kids. I've set up family banks for two of the Jones children already because they don't want to have to pay the loan back.

The Jones parents' family bank has empowered three huge successes and at least two additional family banks. The Jones parents empowered their children to become financially independent on their own, and the five million dollars that started their family bank has now grown to over ten million dollars.

What is a family bank? A family bank is an estate planning tool that serves three primary purposes. When set up properly, they avoid estate taxes after the death of not only the grantor and spouse, but it is also exempt from estate taxes for future heirs, beneficiaries, and members. Asset protection is the second major benefit of a family bank. Assets are protected from creditors and claimants of the grantors and the beneficiaries. In addition, assets are protected from spendthrifts and attacks from any future ex-spouses of members or beneficiaries. The final objective of a family bank is to provide well defined rules-based access to funds held inside the bank. While loans are generally permitted for a variety of purposes, withdrawals may be constrained to health related and educational expenses.

With kids, you can ignore and hope for the best, you can enable and accelerate the worst, or you can empower and increase the odds for tremendous success. But this last option requires focus and intentionality, and to be intentional about the legacy you leave, you must know what you want that legacy to be. You cannot work toward what you don't have a vision for.

Where do you start? Allow me to suggest taking a look in the rearview mirror.

The legacy you leave your children is far bigger than just you—it either carries on or transforms elements of your own heritage from generations past. You can pass forward and add to the blessings you received from your family and mentors, instill new positive principles and values, break generational curses, and transform destructive thinking patterns no matter how long they've existed in your family.

Legacy is not about what handouts get distributed after you are gone. It is about honoring the hard work and sacrifice that you and your ancestors have made to forge a better life for the ones you love. I encourage you to think about what legacy means to you and your family. I have found that for many of my clients it's the desire to launch the next generation off of their shoulders. Many times, referred to as hand ups and not handouts.

So let me ask, what good things do you want to pass on? What did you not have that you want to give your descendants? What destructive patterns in your family do you want to end with you?

One of the values my father passed to me is risk taking. He lives with an entrepreneurial mindset and a spirit of adventure and believes boldly in the idea that it's better to try and fail than to regret never trying at all. As I grew up under his wing,

I learned to value the principle of risk myself, and now, it's something I intentionally seek to teach and encourage in my own kids' lives.

Maybe your father was a mechanic who taught you the values of grit and hard work. Maybe your mother was a teacher and taught you the value of education and humility. Maybe those are values you want to pass on by setting incentives in place for your kids to experience manual labor and go to college. On the contrary, maybe your father was a workaholic, and your mother was overprotective, and to reverse those effects in your family, two of the values you want to instill moving forward are quality time and liberty.

Whatever your story, understanding where you come from can give you direction in moving forward. You may not be able to choose your heritage, but you do get to choose your legacy.

A series of questions to consider as you begin to design your legacy:

- What do I want my family to stand for?

- What do I value?

- What do I want to add to my values that I haven't so far?

- Who would I like to become?

- What do I want to help my heirs and descendants become?

- What are my greatest assets, material or not?

- What relationships do I have that I want to share with my kids?

- What role does money or success have in my life?

- How important is generosity in my life, and what does that mean?

- Why am I successful?

- What can I begin to change now to create my legacy?

At Legacy Planning Partners, our goal is to help you build your own legacy plan based on your core values and vision. To help in that process, we use a tool provided by one of our partners in planning, The Cedar Gate. They have a deck of fifty-two cards, each with a different value. That may sound overwhelming, but it works. We lay those cards out and have the client pick ten values to which they most identify. Next, we have them eliminate one card at a time until it narrows down to five or six cards. Those final cards identify their family's core values.

From there we help our client craft a family vision statement. It's a paragraph made up of four to five sentences, usually made up of the values whittled down from the deck of values cards. It's a powerful moment when a family understands that their entire mission as a family is united. It allows for a family to make important decisions that impact their business and personal lives, keeping clear on the "why." Once we have that foundation in place, we can move forward to make sure it stays strong.

Our company plans to create relationships with clients that are lifelong. Because of this, we check and recheck with our clients every year on how their Legacy Plan is evolving.

One of the most important parts of intentionally building a legacy is not just talking about your values but living out what you want to see replicated in your next generations.

One of the most satisfying parts of my life is to observe my own children building their Legacy Plan. They started much earlier than I did. To see my children begin constructing their own family banks in their twenties fills me with such pride. My life had to *show* my kids not just *tell* my kids what I valued. I am very aware that I could talk and talk to my kids about legacy and the value of living a life of deeper meaning than chasing money, but I've also lived intentionally in ways that give an example. It's kind of like that old saying "preach, and when necessary, use words."

Clarity came when my daughter asked me to review her income tax return before filing. I was struck by how much money she had given that year. Her giving far surpassed what is mentioned in the Bible, the ten percent tithe. It wasn't because I told her, "Honey, you need to be giving." It was because our family believes in unconditional love.

What is unconditional love? It is love that's bigger than a person's actions or behaviors. It's a love that says, "We may not love what you did last night. We might even be disappointed in your actions right now. But you? We love." And in the end, a legacy of love leads to generosity.

What a proud moment for me as a dad, to realize the living legacy I've been working to pass on is working. When you do what is right consistently, you will see results. Not always immediately, but eventually.

Have you ever heard the saying "The proof is in

the pudding"? This means that the real worth, or effectiveness of something can only be determined by putting it to the test, not just by looking at it. All these things I talk about regarding legacy and values are put to the test in my life by the results of my family. When I see my children operating in generosity and kindness and when my kids put into practice the art of serving others first, that is the "proof" of what my legacy means. It shows me we're right on track.

How can you live today in a way that communicates the values you want to leave behind tomorrow?

# Chapter 3
# Impact

Whether big or small, every single one of us impacts the world and plays a part in determining the future that comes after us. This is what Bob Buford, author of *Half Time,* calls "significance." He explains, "Success means using your knowledge and experience to satisfy yourself. Significance means using your knowledge and experience to change the lives of others."

I have seen friends and clients use their influence, wealth, and legacy to transform culture and leave the world a better place than they found it. Sometimes this happens on a global scale to end the international water crisis, sometimes it happens on a local level with inner-city development projects, and sometimes it happens on a personal level inside a family. In each case, I would argue that this is the kind of legacy that matters in the end—not just that you set your kids up to succeed, but that you set them up to make a difference in the world. A healthy legacy should provide maximum opportunity for greatness and minimize the likelihood of ruin.

But how do you do that when your kids are already heading down a destructive path?

Twenty years ago, I would have told you that you can't roll back time and un-rotten the apple. But now, my perspective has changed. I have witnessed through some of the Legacy Planning we have done that people really can change.

A prime example is a family I worked with on a Legacy Plan a few years ago. The parents had four kids, three of whom were all successful ranchers, farmers, and entrepreneurs. They all went out and built their own lives, except for the youngest son. He never launched.

My first impression of the youngest son was during a Legacy Planning meeting. Our meeting location was down a two-and-a-half mile stretch of dirt road, which led to a blacktop in front of a large metal building the family owned. The kids had come to be a part of constructing a mission statement, which would serve as the preamble for their family constitution. Two of the four kids, a son and daughter, were already there. As we sat talking for a few minutes, one of the other sons who owned a trucking company called to say he had a crisis at work and wouldn't be able to come. This left us waiting on the youngest son.

Apparently the youngest was sleeping in, as was his custom. We started the meeting without him. As we talked, I noticed movement out of the corner of my eye in the direction of the window. Dirt was flying through the air behind a Corvette racing down the road, tires squealing as the car hit the blacktop. It was going so fast, I braced for impact! The driver managed to stop it just in time and I realized it was the youngest son. He had decided to join us. He jumped out of the car, sunglasses on, and plopped down at the table with us looking like a mess. He never took his sunglasses off.

During our next meeting, we went over the family bank without the kids. As you can imagine, the father was extremely concerned that his youngest son would blow any money that was left to him, so I suggested an idea to deal with the entitlement mindset of such a young man. I suggested that they set up their own foundation and put the youngest son in charge of the giving. Remember, a healthy legacy should "maximize the opportunity for greatness." That's what I was hoping this would do. Further, we would also put him in charge of vetting all the donation requests.

When a foundation goes live to receive requests, charities try to get in on the ground floor. As one of their original recipients, many times that leads to being a recipient for life. I knew this would mean immediate work for this young man. With each request he would have to find out: Is this a real charity? How important is the work the charity does? Do they waste money or spend their money wisely? After researching all the necessary information, he would have to present to the family where the money should go. This allowed for the family to hold him accountable. And they did.

As a result, six months later, the family decided they had their Legacy Plan set and could handle things on their own. They didn't need me to hold their hand, so to speak. Three years later, we got the whole family together again to review their plan and discuss some new tools for them to try.

Driving down that same dirt road towards the same metal building, someone drove behind me in a pickup I didn't recognize. We both stopped at the metal building and stepped out of our vehicles. As the person behind me pulled his sunglasses off, I recognized it was the youngest son. He was cleaned shaven with cut hair and looked like a completely different person.

During the meeting I asked him what the most valuable thing he'd experienced or learned from having a Family Legacy Plan.

"Well, it changed my life," he said matter-of-factly.

He went on to say that he didn't realize just how spoiled rotten he'd really been. He didn't realize he was a jerk until he started reading all the heartbreaking stories of broken families and people whose basic needs were not met. All of that opened his eyes to how his life was so good in comparison. And further, the ability to help them challenged him to grow as a person himself.

Over the course of three years, this Legacy Plan made a tremendous impact on the family. This young man changed his character and left the partying lifestyle. Instead, he saw a purpose for his life through his family. He realized that many great causes were depending on his family to stay successful, which included him.

A lesson for the road: generosity impacts the giver as much as the recipient.

David Green, founder and CEO of Hobby Lobby, shares in his book *A Generous Life:*

"If a generous life is one that leaves a legacy, we

would be remiss not to include our children in conversations about giving. Now that our children are older we practice generosity as a family. We meet together regularly to discuss our giving opportunities and decide where to give. Each request is viewed through our two criteria of eternal: Will it advance God's Word? Will it save a person's soul?

We involve the whole family in this process, both myself and Barbara, as well as our children. Our grandchildren have opened their own donor-advised fund and started their own quarterly meetings where they decide where to give as a family. Involving the younger generations in our decisions on where to give has been essential in passing on our value of generosity."

I believe generosity is essential to legacy. It is a key component of significance. It is the primary component of my own significance. One of the primary missions for me is to live my life as a great example for all the future members of my family. And part of that is ensuring my success is used for significance by helping those in need and launching my kids to do the same.

Zig Zigler used to say, "The more you give, the more you get." I've found that to be true. It's not the reason I give, but it is one of the results. I've met a lot of Christians who don't believe God intends to bless us financially while on earth. They feel like their earthly existence must be painful and punishing in order to serve Jesus well. Not so! (If you are not a Christian, I want you to know my goal is not to badger you with my faith. We can all learn from the principles of the Bible no matter our personal conviction on its validity.)

I heard one of my clients say that he gives, then he expects. He said that he has done his part and he expects God to come through as He promises. *Expects* can be a hard word to grasp sometimes. I had trouble with that for a minute, but the more I thought about it, I realized that it's exactly what the Bible challenges us with in Malachi 3:10: "Bring the full tithe into the storehouse, that there may be food in my house. And thereby put me to the test, says the LORD of hosts, if I will not open the windows of heaven for you and pour down for you a blessing until there is no more need."

This does not mean that God is a vending machine in which you insert a thousand dollars and withdraw ten thousand. What it does mean is that God is faithful, and he loves to honor our trust and obedience, whether that's by expanding our territory in terms of finances, relationships, influence, vision, or peace and joy. I dare you: try to *out-give* God!

Most people are waiting to get before they give. In God's Kingdom, it's the opposite. You give first. Then you receive. I believe part of the reason is to teach us the blessing of giving. The Bible calls us to stand for goodness and justice, to correct oppression, and to fight for the fatherless and the widows (Isaiah 1:17). To *love* and *serve* is the point; to receive is a wonderful side effect.

If you're still unsure about this, let me share a personal story.

When COVID-19 hit, my first inclination was to

back off on my tithing to my church. I thought it might be a good idea to have some cash available in my account "just in case." My natural first response, seeing what was going on in the United States, was to stop spending money and to stop giving money, or at least reduce my giving amount. How many others felt the same?

But then I remembered one of my core beliefs: "The more you give the more you get." If I really believe that, then if I decrease my giving, what else decreases? My getting! What I ended up doing was just the opposite of my first reaction: I increased my giving at the beginning of the quarantine.

Of course, I realize some people might say that sounds stupid, but my blessings haven't stopped.

Please understand, I'm not advocating to *spend* all of your money. There is a difference between giving and spending. When the 2020 COVID-19 quarantine began in the United States, I was prepared to tighten my spending. For example, I decided I was not going to buy a new boat this year, as I had planned before COVID. I didn't know what the future held or how long the effects of COVID would last, and in the face of so many unknowns, I chose to be fiscally responsible.

I believe that God always blesses us in response to our trust. Does He always bless us financially? No, I don't think so. But what if in response to our tithing God's blessing was a new opening of influence or a new opportunity? Would I still trust Him? Yes, because He knows more than I know. I would expect something much greater is meant for me later. I believe God aligns the perfect answer at the perfect moment.

This book isn't to convince you to become a Christian, but I hope we can all learn the same principle together: give first.

When your focus turns to *living* your legacy rather than only leaving it behind, it helps you learn to be satisfied with the simple. Enjoying the journey is not a new thought. Most of us have heard that term at various times. Most of those we hear it from are people we consider older and wiser, toward the end of their journey.

But we can start today. We don't have to wait until we're at the end of the road to celebrate the legacy of our life. A mindset of generosity and gratitude will help you see what's important now. When your mind is focused on money and acquiring things, you'll always be searching for the next deal or the next thing. But when your mind is focused on generosity and gratitude, you will walk in the peace and joy of the moment.

# Chapter 4
# Family Harmony

A good Legacy Plan should alleviate the likelihood, if not completely eliminate the possibility, of heirs fighting over money. That is one of the core reasons we believe in legacy planning: we want families to stay connected and for great-grandchildren to know and love each other.

How do you build teamwork and deeper relationships between family members? Again, there is no option to buy teamwork—it takes focused intentionality.

In my own family, every year we have a Legacy Retreat. What seems to be happenstance during this time is actually all by design. For example, a few years ago, we went whitewater rafting in two-man kayaks down the Royal Gorge River. Rather than riding with whoever they wanted, all the kids were paired across families with one of their cousins, because someday they would be running the family foundation or bank together. Learning teamwork in small ways while young will lay the foundation for it in bigger ways later in life.

One of the things my father does at these retreats is to put the youngest child in charge of the family foundation gifts. This starts when they are ten or eleven years old. A month before the retreat, we link two cousins together and give them each a stack of requests that has come into the foundation. Both kids are given their own packets which have about eight requests. In the time building up to the retreat, they communicate with each other about the charities on the table. Together, they narrow it down to two charities. After their decisions are final, they spend time practicing their presentation on each other and then finally present it to grandma and grandpa at the retreat for them to make the final decision.

Several lessons are learned out of that experience. One of them is discernment. Out of eighteen tragic stories, they have to be narrowed down to the two most deserving. That can make someone feel guilty because it's not that the others weren't deserving. A decision then must be made on what is the best for our family as well. A lot of growth comes from it all.

The first lesson is relationship building between the cousins. We don't pair the same cousins together all through the trip. We want to make sure they move around between cousins of all ages.

Building confidence is another lesson I've witnessed first-hand. My son was an extremely shy child. Everywhere he went, he would hide behind either mine or his mom's legs. One year, he was given the exercise of having to present the charity options to grandma and grandpa at our retreat. He begged me to get out of it, but I didn't budge. I told him that I understood he might not like being in front of people, but he would get better at it. Today, years later, he can make a presentation in front of his entire church. The fact is, he's still a reserved person. It didn't change his personality. But it did help to build a skill that he could use the rest of his life.

This kind of family interdependence helps us to understand that we are surrounded by others who stand for what we stand for and that our families have our back. This kind of interdependent trust eliminates disunity and creates unity. When we share responsibilities and burden, we also share blessings and confidence. We win as a team and as a family. We should all help carry each other's burdens and successes along the way.

When I read Steven Covey's book, *The 7 Habits of Highly Effective People*, it changed my life. Out of the seven principles of the book, the one that stood out to me the most was "Begin With the End in Mind." Meaning live, act, and plan according to where you want to end up someday. This challenged the way I saw my own life and legacy, and I hope it can challenge yours.

Dream with me. When you're old and gray, where do you want to be in relationship with your family? Spending time with your grandchildren or great-grandchildren? Paying the way on family vacations? Continuing in a close relationship with your kids?

One of the best parts of a legacy is enjoying it freely and abundantly while you're still here, and, if I can be frank, one of the primary deterrents I've found to happy, open relationships between families and grandparents is financial dependence. Yes, that can mean when our adult kids or grandchildren are unhealthily financially dependent on us. We will address that more in the next two chapters. However, what it can also mean is being financially dependent on *them*. Prolonged, unhealthy financial dependence on either side can eventually lead to all kinds of conflict of interest, neediness, and avoidance of conversation and interaction.

It's easy as well-off adults with many years still ahead of us to gloss over the idea of ever being financially dependent on our children. Trust me, I get it. However, when poor planning meets even just one unforeseen catastrophe in life, I see reverse dependency on kids happen more than you'd think.

Will you plan for financial stability when you're

old, not just financial freedom when you're young to middle age?

As we get older, myself included, we have to change our mindset to look ahead at what our parents and even grandparents are going through. If you split up the wealth now and end up needing some of it later, it's very hard to get it back. For example, I've seen some people give all their wealth away to their kids, who went out and spent it all. They weren't thinking ahead to the idea of possibly needing extensive medical help and assisted living for the last five years of life due to dementia. It's expensive—and isn't covered by Medicare.

Over the years, courtroom television shows have become famous by bringing in divided families and letting the world watch them sue each other over money. What a sad situation to have a family torn apart after a loved one dies, all because money wasn't handled properly in the beginning.

Part of why we at Legacy Planning Partners are intentional about family legacy is to prevent family fights. Splitting up wealth never goes well. There is an alternative, which is what we do best: we create the family bank. Remember, this gives everyone access to the money without giving the money to someone directly.

I recommend to my clients to leave money in the family bank, so they won't be saddling their kids with the burden of care. With many entrepreneurs, they think they can keep rolling the dice. If they lose some money here and there, they always feel like they can get it back. If someone is in their late sixties and they lose a significant amount, there isn't enough time and energy to gain it back.

# Chapter 5
# Entitlement

Legacy is built on empowerment, not entitlement. Empowerment supercharges our motives. It is like gasoline on the fire. Entitlement, on the other hand, is born from enabling. David Green of Hobby Lobby sums it up in his book *A Generous Life:*

"I simply don't believe that unearned money helps grow the kind of responsible, motivated, focused offspring we all desire. As a parent, I would tell my children, 'The hardest thing for me is to not do something for you.' I would see them struggling, and I wanted to step in and take over, but I knew they needed to learn on their own. When we really love our kids, we need God's wisdom to know how to help them handle money. We simply must raise kids and grandkids to be independent. Otherwise, we make cripples out of them."

In this chapter, we will focus on understanding entitlement, the damage it causes, and how to avoid it. In the next chapter, we will dive into what it means to empower.

I've dealt with many entitled clients through the years. One story that immediately comes to mind is about a lady in central Oklahoma. She had some money to invest and was referred to me.

At the time, she was sixty-five years old, and after investing the money for her, we did her analysis. I told her she would need more for her retirement. She explained that her mom, who was eighty-five at the time, had tons of money that would all go to her when she passed away, so she wasn't worried about it. She went on to explain that with the money she was investing and her Social Security, she would be fine until the passing of her mom. After all, she was eighty-five so it wouldn't be that long.

This woman had all kinds of big dreams and plans for what she was going to do with the money her mom would leave her. She told me all about them. What do you think happened? Did her dreams come true?

Last year, my client's mother died at the age of 105. My client had died the year before her mother, at age eighty-five—twenty years after telling me her mom would die any day and leave her a bunch of money. That was entitlement backfire.

I can't tell you how many times in the past thirty-five years that someone has told me they don't need to plan for retirement or invest for financial independence. The reason they give most often is that their family is so wealthy and that when so-and-so dies, they will get all the money, so they don't need to preplan. When I hear that, it really makes my stomach turn.

My reason for feeling so upset when someone tells me that narrative is that they are putting off experiences they could have funded with their own money. Using discipline and preparation for retirement could have blessed so many people by simply pursuing financial independence.

So, what creates entitlement?

Sometimes, it's useful to look at the antithesis of a Legacy Plan and a family bank. There is no shortage of tragic stories involving famous American heirs becoming victims of a dynasty trust. These generation skipping transfer tax exempt trusts are fantastic estate tax avoidance tools, which is why they are used. Anything you and I put in a dynasty trust doesn't die when we do and therefore it is not subject to a death tax.

Unlike living trusts, typically, dynasty trusts do not get divided up. Instead, these trusts stay invested and distributes income to beneficiaries. Usually, when the recipient reaches a certain age, they start getting a check in the mail either monthly, quarterly, or annually. The philosophy was created for the right reasons, but no one thought about the repercussions. Here's what we see is all too often the case:

A grandfather builds a dynasty trust for the benefit of all the grandkids and great-grandkids. The reasoning generally revolves around the idea that the wealth inside the living trust will be distributed to the next generation at the death of the wealth creator. The wealth inside the dynasty trust stays invested and continues to grow for many years before distributions begin. On face value, this makes a lot of sense. In reality, trusts created twenty or thirty years ago and invested for growth may now be worth many millions of dollars more than originally expected. In turn, the distributions from the trust that were expected to be modest supplements to income turn into ambition stifling dollar amounts.

Consider the following example:

An entrepreneur and his spouse contribute two million dollars in assets to a dynasty trust for the benefit of their four grandchildren with five percent distributions to begin in twenty-one years. Assuming a five percent growth rate, the trust account would have grown to around six million dollars and would provide 75,000 dollars a year to each grandchild. However, the trust earned closer to ten percent and instead has a value close to sixteen million dollars with annual distributions of

200,000 dollars a year for each beneficiary. While 75,000 dollars would be a meaningful supplement to a young family's income, 200,000 dollars might encourage slothfulness and diminish their drive to be successful through their own merits.

Most of the clients of our firm are very concerned that their generosity might create an entitlement attitude in their heirs. Just because your last name is Buffett, or Hilton, or Gates should not make you entitled to a life of overindulgence. It's not surprising to see wild side effects of tons of money when a person doesn't have a strong set of core values instilled in them from a young age.

That is the destructive power of enablement—not only that it fuels destructive patterns, but that it steals the dignity and drive of self-accomplishment.

Typically, when meeting with families, I lead them through ideas and plans but the ultimate decision is always theirs. I usually bite my tongue, even when I think they should do something different, unless they specifically ask me. But one time, I had to speak up.

I was dealing with a big ranch family. We had built their Legacy Plan, their family bank, and everything else that goes with it. The next step after that is to have a family meeting and roll the plan out to the kids. But the parents explained they didn't want to do that the first year, so we waited.

The second year rolled around and I was at the family's house and I asked if we were going to have a family meeting that year. The couple looked at each other and shook their heads—no. So once again, no family meeting. The following year, the same thing happened again. At that point, I finally had to say something.

"Let's stop for a minute. There's something I don't understand or that you aren't sharing with me. There has to be a reason why you don't want to roll it out to your kids."

The wife looked at her husband. He nodded.

"It's our daughter and her husband we're concerned about," she said. "As you know, all of our money and land is going into the family bank. Which means the only way to access the money is by application and permission. If someone wants money, they will have to fill out a request, and depending on the request, the loan may have to be paid back."

I nodded. That was how the parents had wanted to set it up.

"Well, we're afraid that once our daughter's husband finds out that they will never get an inheritance outright, he will leave her."

I had to ask the hard question. "Do you believe he only married your daughter for the hope of money?"

"Yes," was their pained response.

"If I can just be honest, here's my opinion: Your daughter is only forty-five years old. If her husband would really leave her after learning about the money, then let's get it over with now. Why would you want to wait another twenty years? He's going to eventually find out, and better sooner rather than later."

They agreed and we had the family meeting about six months later. Within the month, can you guess what happened? Their daughter's husband filed for divorce and left. But wait, there is a happy ending! Their daughter ended up getting remarried two years later to the guy who owned the land next door to them. He was a great guy that loves her for who she is and not for the land she was going to inherit.

You can see where entitlement played a huge role in the first husband's view of what would automatically be given to *him*, not just to his wife. He felt entitled to it simply because he was married to her.

Another client of mine who built his own company had one child—a daughter. Although I dealt some with her throughout the years, the father was my main client. She never worked, nor did she have anything to do with her father's company. All of her money came from her father. When he passed away, she inherited the company. In three years, she turned a ten million dollar company into a two million dollar company and had to sell it.

When she came to me with her two million dollars, I had proposed she consider an investment with an income guarantee that would have provided her with a sizable monthly income that she could not outlive. But she was hesitant. Instead of putting all two million dollars in, she put 500,000 dollars and kept the other 1.5 million accessible to her because she had some things she wanted to take care of. She told me after a year she would bring the rest of the money in to invest.

Unfortunately, she met an investment guy that year who promised her the moon and everything in between. She ended up getting into options and other high-risk investments. You guessed it. By the time she turned things around, she had lost over half her money.

Only a small fraction of people are educated to handle

that kind of wealth, and either they fall prey to some-one lying to them and actually taking their money or they lose it all in bad investments.

If you leverage your wealth and things turn against you, you lose it all.

That's why our family banks have investment policies. You can take risks—aggressive risks even—with one percentage of your portfolio as long as you're not lever-aging the other ninety-nine percent. Establishing sucn cinct investment policies can help you safeguard your wealth from unscrupulous people who don't care about you and only want your money.

So, now that we understand the damage of entitlement and enablement, what can we do instead? I'm glad you asked. The answer is *empowerment*.

# Chapter 6
# Empowerment

What's the difference between enabling and empowering? Enabling is helping your child stay lazy, empowering is helping them accomplish goals.

How then do you move from enabling to empowering? First, your child needs to have goals. And how do you give rise to goals, you wonder? Dreams.

Pastor Craig Groeschel of Life Church often says that, "Everyone ends up somewhere, few end up somewhere on purpose." This illustrates the idea of what it means to live with *purpose, goals,* and *dreams.* Dreams have the remarkable power to move us to action. What are your kids' dreams? What are you hoping and living for? What passions and burdens weigh in their heart? When our kids become driven on their own, that's when we as parents get to step in and help support our kids in what they are pursuing rather than enabling them to stay put and go nowhere.

My dream for my family is for them to become all that *God* wants them to be. I want them to love their family like I love them. I want them at a younger age to feel as blessed as I feel now. And I hope they will be ignited with massive generosity.

I think very few of us feel we have arrived at the perfect place in life. Most of us think about ways we can improve things. We picture our perfect family or our perfect future. Dreams are important! Once you have your dream, you map it. With focus, you can turn that dream into a vision and that becomes a plan. Once you write that plan and give yourself measurable outcomes with real deadlines, you can turn your dream into reality.

People don't plan to fail, they fail to plan. Harvard Business School has been studying their MBA graduates for the last thirty years. Three percent of graduates who had their goals written down ended up earning more than the other ninety-seven percent put together. There were even some ten year periods where the three percent earned ten times more than the other ninety-seven percent.

Empowerment comes from turning dreams into goals, and goals into plans. Most people dream, some visualize it, but only a few plan it. When you plan it, everything changes. Let's go through a couple of empowerment examples.

One family client of mine who I think really hit empowerment out of the park is the Hill family. Brian and Marla Hill have every ability to gift their kids with brand new cars on their sixteenth birthdays, but when their oldest son, Holden, was finally old enough to drive, they decided to take a different approach.

While reading the book of Proverbs with his son, Brian Hill took special notice of King Solomon's teaching in Proverbs 24:6: "for by wise guidance you can wage your war, and in the abundance of counselors there is victory." Holden had just turned sixteen-years-old and was looking for opportunities to earn money for buying a vehicle. Brian, rather than helping his son find a job or offering him a job in his company, took inspiration from Salomon and challenged his son with an idea: ask for meetings with and interview a multitude of successful, impactful leaders, and learn from them. I'll pay you fifty dollars per interview. Each interview has to be accompanied by a one page written summary of what you learned. As Brian would say, "I can either pay my kids to stack boxes, or I can pay them to do something that will be truly impactful for them. I'd rather do the second."

Holden agreed, pulled in by the prospect of such a cool project for one, and also, the reward of earning a vehicle. He decided on his own goal of 500 interviews, which would earn him 25,000 dollars.

Over the next two years, Holden ended up traveling the breadth of the United States and meeting hundreds of recognizable leaders from across the country and around the world, and he earned his 25,000 dollars. But what is particularly cool about how the story ends is that Holden decided to use his earnings for something other than a car—instead, he opted to hire a professional writing coach and editor to walk him through the journey of writing his own book titled *Bring the Fire*. Brian was greatly encouraged by Holden's personal and professional growth after the past year and admired his decision to pour his funds into something lasting and significant rather than a brand new sports car. Brian decided to reward Holden by buying him a reasonable vehicle.

Holden was just the first. Each of his siblings have undertaken similar journeys to earn their own vehicle, and each one of them has grown into a passionate, dedicated, well-refined leader themselves. This is the effect of what we call, "empowerment."

Over the years, we have had the privilege of learning unique ways our clients have empowered their children to be all that they can be. One example that comes to mind starts at the early age of what most call "an allowance." Most of us that give an allowance do so because they complete chores and tasks around the house/ranch/company. Changing the term "allowance" to "pay or compensation" changes the narrative from you get this because your part of our family to you get this because you have worked for it.

Here is another story from a great friend, Ross Hill, on empowerment. He tells the story like this.

"We want our kids to be completely self-sufficient by the time they go off to college, start a job, become an adult and live independently from home. And it's too late to start training them once they're eighteen, so we start at the age of twelve.

One of the things we do is give the children a clothing budget. Two times a year we have them take an inventory of everything they have to wear. Then they will decide what they're going to buy, what they have to replace, jeans, underwear, socks, t shirts, sweatshirts, whatever. We give them an allotted amount of money to spend. We take them to the store and they buy their clothes for the fall school semester, then right between Christmas and New Year's they will buy their clothes for the spring semester. And whatever they buy is what they have.

One time, our son decided he was going to buy a 110 dollar pair of Lucky jeans. So, he ended up with only one pair of jeans for the fall semester. We also have the children be responsible for doing their own laundry, which meant our son was having to do his laundry all the time and the washing machine was causing his jeans to become threadbare, and the pockets were pulling apart. He was very upset with us because we wouldn't give him any more money and we said, 'Well, buddy, the amount of money you had was up to you to spend how you wanted. You knew Lucky's were at least two times as expensive as what any other jeans would cost and you decided you had to have those. Now, you have to live with your decision. Next year, you'll get another chance.'

Guess what: today, years later, our son has perfect credit. In fact, all of our kids do, because they learned to budget their money and live with their mistakes when they were young, and we were there to help them, coach them, and not bail them out of their mistakes.

Something to learn is that when you bail your kids out of their mistakes all the time, they just keep making them, because they don't have to live with the consequences of their decisions. You need to let them experience the sting of their choices. It works!"

Here's a personal story of empowerment told by my daughter who joined our firm five years ago:

"Growing up I was involved in agriculture projects and basketball. My parents were big on my brother and I finding our love and passion over and above their own hopes for us. For me, showing cattle was my love. Sure,

I enjoyed playing basketball, but it was always a deterrent when I would miss a game to attend a cattle show and then be benched during the following game.

Finally, I asked my dad if he was okay with me showing cattle as my full-time extracurricular activity. Going to him with this question made me overly nervous. Much to my surprise, he was very supportive and said that I could come to the Chaney family bank for any loans that I may need in this endeavor. In that moment, my family showed the support and empowerment I needed to change the shape of the rest of my life.

Dad put me into contact with one of his clients who raised show cattle. I visited with them, sorted through their herd, and picked out my first show heifer, Suede. Through this process, I learned how to negotiate and present a business plan to dad and mom. This was the start to an exciting business venture which evolved into an extensive embryo transfer program. A few years into this venture I realized that my facilities needed an upgrade. Once again, I presented a business and repayment plan to my parents. I was tasked with managing the contactors, designing the working facilities, and managing the budget. Talk about empowerment!

By operating my own cattle company, I learned about being responsible for animals that depend on you for care, how to run a company at a young age, how to evaluate risks and rewards, how to lose humbly, and I learned work ethic."

This example is to encourage you to think about what ways you can empower future generations of your family. Maybe it's investing in a lawn mower business for your son/grandson or maybe investing in a Cricut machine for your daughter/granddaughter's passion for making and selling crafts. Whatever their passion is, we encourage you to empower them towards their goals.

# Chapter 7
# True Fulfillment

I am amazed by how many financially successful people are so empty inside. It breaks my heart because it doesn't have to be that way. The truth is, money doesn't make us empty; but it does not fulfill us, either. The crazy thing about true fulfillment is that it comes as a result not of what you get, but of what you give. As we're reminded by Jesus in Acts 20:35, "It is more blessed to give than to receive."

This does not mean you give all you have away—it *might* mean that for you, but not necessarily. If you want to truly experience fulfillment focus on how to use your money to love others. Money is simply a tool. It is neither a blessing nor a curse on its own; what you do with it determines its outcome.

My client, Vince, passed away before the writing of this book, but his story is powerful. Though it seems like yesterday, I helped him and his wife set up their family bank and construct their family constitution almost thirty years ago.

Vince and his wife both came from very large families. One had nine brothers and sisters, the other had eleven. They were both schoolteachers. Their whole life they made very little money. They never had children of their own. They didn't think they could afford to feed and educate them since they were both teachers living on meager salaries. By the time they came into money, they considered having kids, but they were already in their forties.

The couple had been saving money since they were in their early twenties. When he turned forty-five, he asked his wife's permission to buy some land. He explained he had always wanted to own some cattle and live in the country. He felt they had finally saved up enough money to purchase some land outside of town. They ended up buying eighty acres of Western Oklahoma ranch land.

A year and a half after he bought the property, they found oil on his land. This small oilfield overly blessed them and they became extremely wealthy. In his mind, the land would be used to run some cows, but it just happened to be the perfect eighty acres. For many years, just by the fact that he owned the service, his income was between 700-900 thousand dollars a year. Since they were still schoolteachers, as was their habit, they didn't spend any of it.

He had CDs in multiple banks within a 150 mile radius of his ranch. Every year until he died, he would literally get in his truck and drive all day long, renewing his CDs. He didn't have air conditioning in his old truck. I rode with him several times for these CD renewal trips, and I hated those trips during the summer. It would get so hot, especially when we would go into a bank and come out thirty minutes later. The truck would be on fire! We'd drive with the windows down which felt like fire on our face because it was 105 degrees! I was so happy when he finally got a new truck; it was still ten years old, but at least it had air conditioning that worked. Vince also usually wore bib overalls that only had one button left on the bib, so one side was always hanging down. That was just him. He was very frugal.

In lieu of all the superficial things, there are several special things about Vince regarding significance and true fulfillment. Some of it may even blow your mind!

I sat down with Vince shortly after meeting him. I asked him what he wanted to happen with his wealth and where he wanted to make a difference. He answered that there were a couple of things he really wanted to accomplish.

First was regarding his hometown, which he and his wife still visited often. Located on a highway that had a lot of increased traffic, it meant the kids in town had to cross the highway to get to school. Vince explained he wanted to build a crosswalk over the highway where children could walk safely to school. And that's exactly what he did. They also had a new gymnasium built for the school, among other things.

I was particularly intrigued with the estate planning they had done in the eighties before I was even in the business. It was a dynasty trust, he explained, but what he described sounded similar to our family bank in that you had to do something to get the money.

Vince went on to explain how he and his wife wanted to share their financial blessings with their families. They decided they wanted to provide college education opportunities to all of their nieces and nephews. Considering their large extended family, that added up! If the nieces and nephews would go to college and make good grades, they would pay for every semester, every part of it.

His reasoning behind this was that in the late seventies when the oil boom hit Oklahoma, most of his nephews would graduate high school and then go to the oil fields instead of college. They could make a lot of money working the fields at the time, much more than going to college. Shortly before his estate planning, one of Vince's nephews was killed on a rig and he was devastated over it. This was the reason Vince set up the trust the way he did. He would pay 1,000 dollars a month, plus room, board, books, and tuition, for them to go to college. This was the case for twenty years.

Around this time, I took over his account because my dad was slowing down his practice and eager to let me take the lead on clients living over three hours away. When I asked Vince how things were going, he lamented they were having all kinds of nightmares. When the trust was set up, they put an inflation factor to it. So, the original 1,000 dollars a month had increased to 3,000 dollars a month in addition to room, board, books, and tuition.

If a person receives 3,000 dollars a month to go to college, they'd never want to quit. He had nieces and nephews who had been in college for seven and eight years already. All this without anything to show. Of course, this was never set up in order for the kids to stay in college forever. Yet there were no predetermined expectations of graduating, so they went from one major to another and stayed in college.

I brought it up that if I was making 36,000 dollars a year with no expenses, I would probably stay in college for ten years too.

Another unexpected consequence was that some of his family had used the trust to become doctors and lawyers. He personally was not too keen on lawyers. Once they came into wealth, people came out of the woodwork to sue him.

During our meeting over all of these concerns, Vince was unsure about being able to change any of the conditions of the trust. I told him I would read his trust and report back. After reading the trust the dollar amounts were not included in his trust documents. The trust indicated the beneficiaries could have access to the funds in the trust for health, education, maintenance, and wealth fare. I was happy to report back to Vince that he could make all the necessary adjustments to the college education funding amount that he wished.

My suggestion to Vince was that we forget the past and start over. I reminded him that what he had originally intended, which was for all of his nieces and nephews to attend college, had happened. Before the trust, less than half of them went.

When I asked him what would make him feel better about it, he said that he was hoping some of them would become teachers or preachers. He also said he didn't necessarily blame them because there's no money in those professions. Then he said, "But doggone it, there's more to life than money."

He went on to explain that hardly a day would go by that a former student didn't drive out to the panhandle to visit him and his wife and thank them for what they meant to their life when they were teachers.

I can just imagine how wonderful they were as teachers. They were the sweetest, most caring people. They were probably everyone's favorite teacher. Twice while I was there, someone showed up just to let them know that their success was because of them. You can't buy a thank you like that.

As we began to try and make a feasible plan that would include an incentive for those (now) grand-nieces and grand-nephews who might be interested in a career in education or ministry, I asked Vince how much was currently in his trust. The amount was hundreds of millions, and it was making over 10 million dollars a year in interest alone.

I suggested that we create a family rule book to go along with his trust now as our "family constitution" to spell out his and his wife's desires with the family. He proposed a clause that stated if anyone would become a teacher or minister—or another profession Vince and his wife felt was noble, but underpaid—the trust could supplement their income. That way the college degree would not be based on outcome of income, but hopefully a heart-felt profession to benefit others.

After crunching the numbers for him, I realized it wasn't even going to take a third of the interest income he was making each year to fund. I also suggested he back off on the "salary" he paid for just going to college. He could still pay for room, board, books, and tuition, but there was no reason to give more than 500 dollars a month in spending money.

With the family constitution completed there was now an incentive to become a teacher, social worker, minister, etc. Two years later, he had several grand-nieces and nephews studying to become teachers. Why? Because now with the trust, teachers would make a more than adequate income. The last time I checked in with him before he passed, he had close to a dozen family members in the ministry and close to the same number working as teachers, all incentivized by changing the family constitution.

A "family constitution" is your rulebook for your family bank. It outlines how money can be withdrawn, when it can be withdrawn, and how much can be withdrawn. Vince didn't really have a constitution before I met him, but when we made these changes, I introduced the idea of the family constitution. I explained that he wouldn't always be here, and once he's gone, the heirs need to know where the rulebook is and have access to it. The rules can be changed until a person dies, but typically the rules are frozen upon the death of that person. That's a safeguard so the rules can't be changed by the heirs to suit themselves. The person who made all the money gets to make the rules.

With all the heirs, there were hundreds of people that were able to attend college because of Vince's trust. Through this, he stepped into a total sense of satisfaction and fulfillment before he passed away.

What can we learn from Vince's story? First of all, buy an air-conditioned car!

In all seriousness, here's what I hope we learn from stories like his and others I've shared in this book: I think that through Legacy Planning we can put a limit on bad things while completely removing the lid on the limit of good things. I have not witnessed any limits of possibilities and opportunities of good Family Legacy Planning. And the byproduct of this is that it will greatly decrease the odds of all the things that scare us about our success and wealth.

Good Family Legacy Planning eliminates the bad as much as possible. At the same time, you magnify, propel, propagate, fertilize, and water everything you can to increase the abundance of greatness, accomplishment, and values within your family.

Money is not the goal. Impact is the goal. What impact can occur from the legacy that you took the time to build in order to protect your family and the community that you love? Your community could be your church, your town, and, of course, those around you.

The fact is, we're all going to leave a legacy behind. What will yours be?

# Chapter 8
# Touchdown

Can you really use your wealth to leave behind a legacy that guides, brings together, and empowers your descendants for generations to come? I hope the pages of this book have encouraged you to reply with a resounding, "Yes!" Perhaps the question to be asked at this point is, what now?

I want to share a quick story to illustrate how many people believe their children can handle any amount of wealth passed down to them, and then I'll encourage you to think differently.

John came from a family of three children. His parents were Thomas and Mary. He was the middle child, with an older brother named Wes and a younger sister, Julie. His dad ran a very successful family business.

In high school, John didn't make the best life choices. He started running with some of his football buddies, and in the off-season, one of his teammates had a party with no parents at home. They had someone bring alcohol; and then, as if they weren't in enough trouble already, they decided to drive. A group of drunk high schoolers in a pick-up truck never ends well. They wrecked and got arrested. Fortunately for them, they were young enough to get off the hook without a police record.

Around this time, Thomas and Mary had a big overseas trip planned. Taking his wife's advice, Thomas finally decided to get their estate plan in order before the trip. What would happen to their money if they died? Not a big concern, but like many Americans, they decided it was at least worth an afternoon's attention.

Thomas and Mary were comfortable with passing Wes and Julie their third of the inheritance, but John was a concern.

So, they decided to leave the money in a trust with restrictions, incentives, and rules for accessing money.

For example, John might be allowed to withdraw money to fix his car or borrow money to buy a house, but not allowed to withdraw money for extravagant purchases or funding undesirable behavior.

With a few quick questions and strokes of a pen, their planner helped them build a trust to protect John from himself, and unrestricted access for Wes and Julie where they would receive their third of the inheritance out-right with no limits or rules. Unlike John, Wes had been very responsible, and Julie was their rule-follower, so Thomas and Mary thought precautions were unnecessary for them.

What do you think happened when Thomas and Mary went on their overseas trip? Nothing. They had a great time. When they got home, life continued on as usual and the estate plan stayed in place without any discussion among the family. None of the three adult children were even aware of the details of the estate plan.

As John grew older, he began to get back on course in his life, went to college, and became a hard-working young man.

Tragically, one night the parents died in an auto accident. Nothing in their estate plan had been developed more than that one afternoon spent on it many years ago during a rough patch in John's life. When it came time to give the kids their portion, Wes and Julie were given their third, and John's portion (despite him transforming his life) was still set up to go into a trust.

What happened to Wes, Julie, and John?

For a while, Wes led the company well, Julie settled down and got married, and John went to college and started building his own company. Then, the storm hit.

Wes hit an intense patch of marriage problems and his abundant wealth, which had been handed to him without him having to build the emotional and mental fortitude to handle it, crushed him. He lost control of his life to alcohol and affairs, crashed his marriage in an ugly divorce, and steered the family business to the brink of bankruptcy.

In the wake of Wes's collapsing life, Julie and her husband (who had also become part owner of the family company) bought Wes's share of the company and managed to save it from falling off the edge.

What happened to John? When their parents died and

he learned his third of the inheritance was to be placed in a trust, he struggled at first, knowing that his father's decision was based on old distrust that had long been restored. But in the long run, the built-in incentives of the trust ended up leading John into an even better future. Over the years, he built his multi-million dollar company and is now far more successful than anyone in his family. What he resented at the time ultimately helped him to create a path of patience and responsibility in building his own wealth.

To this day, John is a very successful entrepreneur, Julie and her husband run the family company, and sadly, Wes has gone off the rail, is still lost to his devices, and rarely sees the family anymore.

So, what can we learn? Were Thomas and Mary wrong about Wes in assuming he was a stable, smart, and good-hearted man capable of handling a large inheritance? I don't think so. Was his influx of wealth the reason he hit a bunch of marriage problems and lost control of his life? I don't think that's necessarily the case, either. So, if Wes was a strong, stable person, and if his marriage problems were prone to happen whether he inherited a lot of wealth or not, where did their parents go wrong?

I believe Thomas and Mary made the same mistake that many families in America make: they left their legacy *vulnerable*.

Well-intentioned parents will leave an inheritance to their kids, but won't spend the proper time and care to plan for and protect the values of that inheritance. Now, it's fair to ask, would established rules and restraints on the wealth Wes inherited have prevented his marriage problems? Well, possibly—finances are in fact the number one cause for marriage problems and divorce in the United States. Certainly, he may have experienced all the same personal problems regardless of his parents planning. However, in the very least, proper planning on his parents' part would have drastically minimized the damage Wes caused and reduced his self-destructive tailspin.

Imagine with me for a moment that your family is a football team and you're the team captain and quarterback with the ball in your hands. Now, here's a question: Would you be wise to send your kids onto the field without pads, helmets, gloves, and cleats? What about without proper training and regular practices to keep them strong, flexible, and skilled? What about without strong and skilled teammates to help block and protect their path? What about without an experienced coach overseeing the team to call plays, see and address problems, and strategize for a successful pass and touchdown?

Now, if you get all that right, does that mean your kids are invincible? No, but it does set them up for success.

You are the quarterback; the ball is in your hands. At Legacy Planning Partners, we help you build a strong team, deliver a successful pass, and land the touchdown—passing your legacy.

Today, John—the rebel teenager turned successful entrepreneur—is now one of our greatest clients and we have helped him build a family bank trust, a family legacy trust, and all the things that we do discussed in this book. John is the poster child of all the things you should do. And even though he was at first resentful of the incentive trust that he felt handcuffed by in his younger life, he'll be the first to admit now that it was the greatest gift his father ever gave him.

Our clients don't want to cut their kids off, but they do have fears about what might happen to their kids if they were to suddenly inherit millions of dollars without any kind of plan. We all want to protect our kids from hardship in life. However, as most of us have learned, sometimes it's exactly those difficulties that help us to grow and learn. This isn't saying to put hardship on our kids, but that putting a plan in place to pass down our values is equally as important as the financial portion.

One of the things I've pointed out many times throughout my career is that traditional estate planning is broken. Most estate planners are attorneys. This doesn't make them bad, but it does tend to make the process of planning overly simplistic. Estate planners often follow a generic formula rather than truly tailoring the plan for the client. Traditional estate plans tend to read like a laundry list of, "who gets what, when I die." One person gets the fine china, one person gets the coin collection, and the money is divided equally.

What I've seen happen over and over is when a parent is concerned about giving all of their inheritance at one time to a child or other family member, for whatever reason, the attorney will section it off. When the child (or heir) turns thirty, they get a certain amount, when they turn thirty-five, they get another amount, and then when they turn forty, they get the final third.

Sounds good, right? But here's what I've seen time and time again: when the heir gets their first chunk of money at thirty, by the time they are about to turn thirty-five, they've spent every bit of the first round. Now they know another chunk is coming and they know that when they turn forty there will be one more. They've learned how to work the bank, because they're smart. So, they go to a bank and get a loan against the next amount. Now, by the time they turn forty, when that final chunk of money comes in, they've already spent it, or owe it to other people. They've squandered all of their money and now they are broke. It's a sad scenario.

Here's the thing. I've had clients say what you might be thinking, "Well it's not my fault what they do with the money. I'm giving it to them and if they make a mess, then that's theirs to clean up and they can go back to work." All of that might be true. Here's another thought: maybe they should have been working all along, and what if they didn't really need that money at thirty, thirty-five, or forty? What if they're sixty now and they really need it because they might lose their house or business? What if their health is in jeopardy and that money would have helped them with doctor bills?

These are all vital decisions to make when considering who is going to help you plan your legacy. It's not simply about dividing up your assets equally and you're done. There is so much more to it than that.

We offer family legacy planning, family constitution construction, estate tax elimination and minimization strategies, and specialize in implementing strategies to transfer your values to future generations. That's what we build for all of our clients now, who are interested in protecting their value system to make sure that their wealth does not harm their heirs, while making sure they provide them with every opportunity to achieve their own success in life. That's the mantra of what we do at Legacy Planning Partners. Legacy plans do not pass your values—that happens in the context of relationship. What a legacy plan does is guard your values in stressful situations where your values or descendants may be vulnerable.

With our firm, we bring our clients a revelation and observations of how that works. I've been in the business over thirty-five years, and my dad has been in it for over fifty years. To quote Mike Chaney, our founder, "You want to work with us because in the last eighty-five years we have seen everything that works and everything that doesn't work, and our goal is to keep our clients out of the ditches."

How will you be remembered? What foundation will you lay for future generations of your family? What role will your wealth play in empowering your kids for greatness and significance?

If there's one thing I hope you take away from this book, it's this: don't leave it to chance. After all, everyone *leaves* an inheritance, but few put forth the effort to *build* a lasting legacy. I hope you will consider Legacy Planning Partners as the architect to help you build yours.

What will your legacy be?